50 Kid-Friendly Recipes for Home

By: Kelly Johnson

Table of Contents

- PB&J Banana Roll-Ups
- Mini Pita Pizzas
- Rainbow Fruit Kabobs
- Cheesy Veggie Quesadillas
- Ants on a Log (Celery with Peanut Butter and Raisins)
- Mini Veggie Frittatas
- Apple Sandwiches with Granola and Peanut Butter
- Turkey and Cheese Pinwheels
- Veggie Pasta Salad
- Cheesy Broccoli Bites
- Homemade Chicken Nuggets
- Berry Smoothie Popsicles
- Mini Pancake Dippers with Fruit
- Veggie Faces on Crackers
- Veggie Chips (Baked)
- Chocolate Banana Sushi
- Carrot and Hummus Snack Packs
- Crunchy Granola Bars
- Mini Meatball Subs
- Fruit and Yogurt Parfaits
- Veggie Rainbow Wraps
- Mini Corn Dog Muffins
- Cheesy Cauliflower Tots
- Apple Chips (Baked)
- Cheesy Spinach Muffins
- Yogurt Bark with Berries and Granola
- Cucumber and Cream Cheese Sandwiches
- Sweet Potato Fries (Baked)
- Veggie Stuffed Bell Peppers
- Homemade Applesauce
- Mini Chicken Tacos
- Zucchini Pizza Bites
- Cheese and Veggie Quesadilla Dippers
- Trail Mix Energy Bites
- Watermelon Popsicles
- Turkey and Cheese Roll-Ups
- Rainbow Veggie Skewers with Dip
- Veggie Sushi Rolls
- Mini Cheeseburger Sliders
- Fruit Salad with Honey Lime Dressing

- Veggie and Cheese Stuffed Breadsticks
- Frozen Yogurt Bites with Fruit
- Banana Oatmeal Cookies
- Turkey and Veggie Pita Pockets
- Veggie Chips and Salsa
- Homemade Fruit Leather
- English Muffin Pizzas
- Veggie and Ham Breakfast Muffins
- Chicken and Veggie Stir-Fry
- Cheesy Zucchini Fritters

PB&J Banana Roll-Ups

Ingredients:

- 1 large ripe banana
- 2 tablespoons peanut butter
- 2 tablespoons jelly (your choice of flavor)
- 1 large whole wheat tortilla

Instructions:

1. Peel the banana and place it on a cutting board.
2. Spread the peanut butter evenly over one side of the whole wheat tortilla.
3. Spread the jelly on top of the peanut butter, ensuring even coverage.
4. Place the banana horizontally at one edge of the tortilla.
5. Gently roll the tortilla around the banana, pressing lightly to seal the edges.
6. Using a sharp knife, slice the rolled tortilla into bite-sized pieces, about 1 inch thick.
7. Arrange the PB&J Banana Roll-Ups on a plate and serve immediately.

Enjoy these delicious and nutritious roll-ups as a snack, lunchbox treat, or anytime pick-me-up!

Mini Pita Pizzas

Ingredients:

- Mini whole wheat pitas (or regular-sized pitas cut into smaller rounds)
- Pizza sauce
- Shredded mozzarella cheese
- Your choice of toppings (e.g., sliced pepperoni, diced bell peppers, sliced olives, diced tomatoes, cooked sausage, sliced mushrooms, etc.)

Instructions:

1. Preheat your oven to 375°F (190°C).
2. Place the mini pitas on a baking sheet lined with parchment paper.
3. Spread a spoonful of pizza sauce onto each pita, leaving a small border around the edges.
4. Sprinkle shredded mozzarella cheese over the sauce.
5. Add your favorite toppings to each pita.
6. Bake in the preheated oven for about 8-10 minutes, or until the cheese is melted and bubbly.
7. Remove from the oven and let cool for a few minutes before serving.

These Mini Pita Pizzas are perfect for parties, after-school snacks, or even as a quick lunch option. Let your kids get creative with their toppings and enjoy their personalized pizzas!

Rainbow Fruit Kabobs

Ingredients:

- Strawberries
- Mandarin oranges (or segments of clementines)
- Pineapple chunks
- Green grapes
- Blueberries
- Purple grapes
- Wooden skewers

Instructions:

1. Wash all the fruits thoroughly and pat them dry with paper towels.
2. Prepare the fruits by slicing the strawberries, draining any excess liquid from the mandarin oranges, and cutting the pineapple into bite-sized chunks if necessary.
3. Assemble the fruit kabobs by skewering the fruits onto the wooden skewers in rainbow order: start with a grape (purple), followed by a blueberry, then a pineapple chunk, a green grape, a mandarin orange segment, and finally a strawberry.
4. Repeat the pattern with the remaining fruits until all the skewers are filled.
5. Arrange the Rainbow Fruit Kabobs on a serving platter or lay them flat on a plate.

These vibrant and refreshing Rainbow Fruit Kabobs are not only visually appealing but also packed with vitamins and antioxidants. They make a delightful snack for parties, picnics, or simply as a fun way to encourage kids to eat more fruits!

Cheesy Veggie Quesadillas

Ingredients:

- Flour tortillas (medium or large size)
- Shredded cheese (cheddar, mozzarella, or a blend)
- Assorted veggies, diced or sliced (bell peppers, onions, mushrooms, tomatoes, spinach, etc.)
- Olive oil or cooking spray
- Optional: cooked chicken or beans for added protein

Instructions:

1. Heat a non-stick skillet or griddle over medium heat.
2. If using raw veggies, sauté them in a bit of olive oil until they're tender. If using cooked chicken or beans, warm them up in a separate pan.
3. Lay a flour tortilla flat on the skillet or griddle.
4. Sprinkle a generous amount of shredded cheese evenly over half of the tortilla.
5. Add a layer of cooked veggies (and cooked chicken or beans, if using) over the cheese.
6. Fold the empty half of the tortilla over the filling to create a half-moon shape.
7. Cook the quesadilla for 2-3 minutes on each side, or until the tortilla is golden brown and crispy, and the cheese is melted.
8. Repeat the process with the remaining tortillas and filling ingredients.
9. Once cooked, remove the quesadillas from the skillet and let them cool for a minute before slicing them into wedges.
10. Serve the Cheesy Veggie Quesadillas with salsa, guacamole, sour cream, or your favorite dipping sauce.

These Cheesy Veggie Quesadillas are not only tasty but also a great way to sneak in some extra veggies into your kids' diets. They make a perfect lunch, dinner, or even a snack!

Ants on a Log (Celery with Peanut Butter and Raisins)

Ingredients:

- Celery stalks, washed and trimmed
- Peanut butter (or any nut or seed butter of your choice)
- Raisins

Instructions:

1. Cut the celery stalks into manageable lengths, typically about 3-4 inches long.
2. Spread peanut butter (or your chosen nut or seed butter) inside the concave side of each celery stalk.
3. Press raisins into the peanut butter along the length of the celery stalk to resemble "ants on a log." You can line them up in a row or scatter them randomly.

That's it! Your Ants on a Log snack is ready to enjoy. These crunchy, creamy, and slightly sweet treats are perfect for satisfying hunger pangs between meals or as a fun addition to lunchboxes. They're also a great way to introduce kids to different textures and flavors while providing them with a dose of healthy fats, protein, and fiber.

Mini Veggie Frittatas

Ingredients:

- 6 large eggs
- 1/4 cup milk (or non-dairy milk)
- Salt and pepper, to taste
- Assorted veggies, finely diced (such as bell peppers, onions, spinach, tomatoes, mushrooms, etc.)
- Shredded cheese (optional)

Instructions:

1. Preheat your oven to 350°F (175°C). Lightly grease a mini muffin tin with cooking spray or olive oil.
2. In a mixing bowl, whisk together the eggs, milk, salt, and pepper until well combined.
3. Divide the finely diced veggies evenly among the mini muffin cups, filling each cup about halfway.
4. If desired, sprinkle a small amount of shredded cheese over the veggies in each muffin cup.
5. Pour the egg mixture over the veggies and cheese in each muffin cup, filling them nearly to the top.
6. Gently stir the mixture in each muffin cup to ensure the veggies are evenly distributed.
7. Bake in the preheated oven for 15-20 minutes, or until the frittatas are set and lightly golden on top.
8. Remove the mini veggie frittatas from the oven and let them cool in the muffin tin for a few minutes before carefully removing them with a butter knife or spoon.
9. Serve the mini veggie frittatas warm or at room temperature.

These Mini Veggie Frittatas are not only delicious but also packed with protein and veggies, making them a wholesome breakfast or snack option for kids. They can be enjoyed on their own or paired with a side of fresh fruit or whole grain toast for a balanced meal. Plus, they're perfect for meal prep and can be stored in the refrigerator for a few days, making them a convenient grab-and-go option for busy mornings.

Apple Sandwiches with Granola and Peanut Butter

Ingredients:

- 1 large apple, cored and sliced horizontally into rounds
- Peanut butter (or any nut or seed butter of your choice)
- Granola
- Optional: honey, cinnamon, raisins, sliced strawberries, or other toppings of your choice

Instructions:

1. Slice the apple horizontally into rounds, about 1/4 to 1/2 inch thick. Remove any seeds or tough parts from the core.
2. Spread a thin layer of peanut butter (or your chosen nut or seed butter) onto one side of half of the apple slices.
3. Sprinkle granola evenly over the peanut butter on each apple slice.
4. Optionally, drizzle a little honey over the granola for extra sweetness, or sprinkle cinnamon on top for added flavor.
5. If desired, add additional toppings such as raisins, sliced strawberries, or any other toppings of your choice.
6. Place another apple slice on top of each granola-topped apple slice to create "sandwiches."
7. Press gently to secure the sandwich together.
8. Serve the apple sandwiches immediately, or wrap them individually in plastic wrap or store them in an airtight container for later enjoyment.

These Apple Sandwiches with Granola and Peanut Butter are not only delicious but also provide a good balance of protein, fiber, and natural sugars, making them a satisfying and energy-boosting snack for kids. They're perfect for school lunches, picnics, or as a quick and healthy treat any time of the day!

Turkey and Cheese Pinwheels

Ingredients:

- Large flour tortillas
- Sliced turkey breast
- Sliced cheese (cheddar, Swiss, or your favorite cheese)
- Lettuce leaves
- Mayonnaise or cream cheese (optional)
- Mustard (optional)

Instructions:

1. Lay a flour tortilla flat on a clean surface.
2. Spread a thin layer of mayonnaise or cream cheese (if using) over the entire surface of the tortilla.
3. Place a few slices of turkey breast evenly over the tortilla, leaving a small border around the edges.
4. Lay a slice of cheese over the turkey slices.
5. Optionally, add a thin layer of mustard over the cheese (if desired).
6. Place a lettuce leaf on top of the cheese slices.
7. Starting from one end, tightly roll up the tortilla into a log shape.
8. Slice the rolled tortilla into pinwheels, about 1 inch thick.
9. Repeat the process with the remaining tortillas and filling ingredients.
10. Serve the Turkey and Cheese Pinwheels immediately, or wrap them individually in plastic wrap or store them in an airtight container for later enjoyment.

These Turkey and Cheese Pinwheels are not only delicious but also versatile. You can customize them by adding other ingredients such as sliced vegetables (like tomatoes or bell peppers) or switching up the condiments to suit your taste preferences. They make a perfect snack, lunchbox addition, or party appetizer for kids and adults alike!

Veggie Pasta Salad

Ingredients:

- 8 ounces (about 225g) pasta of your choice (penne, rotini, or bowtie work well)
- 1 cup cherry tomatoes, halved
- 1 cup cucumber, diced
- 1 bell pepper (any color), diced
- 1/2 cup red onion, finely chopped
- 1/4 cup black olives, sliced
- 1/4 cup feta cheese, crumbled (optional)
- 2 tablespoons fresh parsley, chopped (for garnish)

For the dressing:

- 1/4 cup olive oil
- 2 tablespoons red wine vinegar
- 1 teaspoon Dijon mustard
- 1 clove garlic, minced
- Salt and pepper, to taste

Instructions:

1. Cook the pasta according to the package instructions until al dente. Drain and rinse under cold water to stop the cooking process. Allow the pasta to cool completely.
2. In a large mixing bowl, combine the cooled pasta, cherry tomatoes, cucumber, bell pepper, red onion, and black olives.
3. In a small bowl, whisk together the olive oil, red wine vinegar, Dijon mustard, minced garlic, salt, and pepper to make the dressing.
4. Pour the dressing over the pasta and vegetables in the large mixing bowl. Toss until everything is evenly coated.
5. If using, sprinkle crumbled feta cheese over the salad and gently toss to combine.
6. Garnish with chopped fresh parsley.

7. Cover the bowl and refrigerate the Veggie Pasta Salad for at least 30 minutes before serving to allow the flavors to meld together.
8. Serve chilled as a refreshing and nutritious side dish.

This Veggie Pasta Salad is not only delicious but also versatile. Feel free to customize it by adding other vegetables, such as broccoli, carrots, or spinach, and adjust the dressing to your taste preferences. It's a great way to enjoy a variety of colorful veggies in one tasty dish!

Cheesy Broccoli Bites

Ingredients:

- 2 cups broccoli florets, steamed until tender
- 1 cup shredded cheddar cheese
- 1/2 cup breadcrumbs
- 1/4 cup grated Parmesan cheese
- 2 eggs
- 2 cloves garlic, minced
- Salt and pepper, to taste
- Olive oil or cooking spray, for greasing

Instructions:

1. Preheat your oven to 375°F (190°C). Grease a baking sheet with olive oil or cooking spray.
2. In a large mixing bowl, mash the steamed broccoli florets with a fork or potato masher until they are finely chopped.
3. Add the shredded cheddar cheese, breadcrumbs, grated Parmesan cheese, minced garlic, eggs, salt, and pepper to the bowl with the mashed broccoli. Mix well until all the ingredients are evenly combined.
4. Using your hands or a spoon, shape the mixture into small bite-sized balls and place them on the prepared baking sheet.
5. Flatten each ball slightly with the palm of your hand to form a bite-sized disc.
6. Bake in the preheated oven for 15-20 minutes, or until the cheesy broccoli bites are golden brown and crispy on the outside.
7. Remove from the oven and let cool for a few minutes before serving.
8. Serve the cheesy broccoli bites warm as a delicious snack or appetizer.

These Cheesy Broccoli Bites are not only packed with flavor but also loaded with nutrients from the broccoli. They make a great addition to lunchboxes, party platters, or as a tasty side dish. Enjoy!

Homemade Chicken Nuggets

Ingredients:

- 1 lb (about 450g) boneless, skinless chicken breasts, cut into bite-sized pieces
- 1 cup breadcrumbs (plain or seasoned)
- 1/2 cup grated Parmesan cheese
- 1 teaspoon garlic powder
- 1 teaspoon paprika
- 1/2 teaspoon salt
- 1/4 teaspoon black pepper
- 2 eggs, beaten
- Cooking spray or olive oil, for greasing

Instructions:

1. Preheat your oven to 400°F (200°C). Grease a baking sheet with cooking spray or olive oil.
2. In a shallow dish, combine the breadcrumbs, grated Parmesan cheese, garlic powder, paprika, salt, and black pepper. Mix well to combine.
3. Place the beaten eggs in another shallow dish.
4. Dip each piece of chicken into the beaten eggs, then coat it evenly with the breadcrumb mixture, pressing gently to adhere.
5. Place the breaded chicken nuggets on the prepared baking sheet, leaving a little space between each piece.
6. Once all the chicken nuggets are breaded and arranged on the baking sheet, lightly spray the tops with cooking spray or drizzle with olive oil.
7. Bake in the preheated oven for 15-20 minutes, flipping halfway through, or until the chicken is cooked through and the coating is golden brown and crispy.
8. Remove from the oven and let cool for a few minutes before serving.
9. Serve the homemade chicken nuggets with your favorite dipping sauce, such as ketchup, honey mustard, or barbecue sauce.

These Homemade Chicken Nuggets are not only delicious but also customizable. You can adjust the seasoning to suit your taste preferences or even try different coatings like crushed cornflakes or panko breadcrumbs for added crunch. Enjoy these crispy nuggets as a healthier version of a classic favorite!

Berry Smoothie Popsicles

Ingredients:

- 2 cups mixed berries (such as strawberries, blueberries, raspberries, blackberries)
- 1 ripe banana
- 1 cup Greek yogurt (plain or vanilla flavored)
- 1-2 tablespoons honey or maple syrup (optional, depending on sweetness preference)
- 1/2 cup milk (dairy or non-dairy)
- Popsicle molds
- Popsicle sticks

Instructions:

1. Wash the mixed berries and remove any stems or hulls.
2. Peel the banana and chop it into chunks.
3. In a blender, combine the mixed berries, banana chunks, Greek yogurt, honey or maple syrup (if using), and milk.
4. Blend the ingredients until smooth and well combined. If the mixture is too thick, you can add more milk to reach your desired consistency.
5. Taste the berry smoothie mixture and adjust the sweetness if needed by adding more honey or maple syrup.
6. Once you're satisfied with the flavor, pour the smoothie mixture into popsicle molds, filling each mold almost to the top.
7. Insert popsicle sticks into the center of each mold.
8. Place the popsicle molds in the freezer and freeze for at least 4-6 hours, or until the berry smoothie popsicles are completely frozen.
9. Once frozen, remove the popsicle molds from the freezer and run them under warm water for a few seconds to help release the popsicles from the molds.
10. Gently remove the berry smoothie popsicles from the molds and serve immediately.

These Berry Smoothie Popsicles are not only delicious but also packed with vitamins, antioxidants, and probiotics from the yogurt. They make a perfect guilt-free treat for kids and adults alike, and you can customize them by using your favorite combination of berries or adding other fruits like mango or pineapple. Enjoy these icy delights as a refreshing snack or dessert!

Mini Pancake Dippers with Fruit

Ingredients:

- Pancake batter (you can use your favorite pancake mix or make it from scratch)
- Assorted fruits (such as strawberries, bananas, blueberries, raspberries)
- Maple syrup or honey, for serving

Instructions:

1. Prepare the pancake batter according to the instructions on the package or your favorite pancake recipe.
2. Heat a non-stick skillet or griddle over medium heat and lightly grease it with butter or cooking spray.
3. Pour small amounts of pancake batter onto the skillet to make mini pancakes, about 2-3 inches in diameter.
4. Cook the mini pancakes for 1-2 minutes on each side, or until they are golden brown and cooked through.
5. While the pancakes are cooking, prepare the fruit by washing and slicing it into bite-sized pieces.
6. Once the mini pancakes are cooked, transfer them to a serving plate.
7. Thread the fruit onto wooden skewers or toothpicks, alternating between different types of fruit.
8. Serve the mini pancake dippers with the fruit skewers on the side, allowing everyone to dip the pancakes into maple syrup or honey and enjoy them with a burst of fresh fruit flavor.

These Mini Pancake Dippers with Fruit are not only delicious but also fun to eat, making them a hit with kids and adults alike. They're perfect for brunch parties or as a special treat for weekend breakfasts. Feel free to get creative with the fruit combinations and toppings to suit your taste preferences. Enjoy!

Veggie Faces on Crackers

Ingredients:

- Crackers (such as round or square-shaped crackers)
- Cream cheese or hummus (for spreading)
- Assorted vegetables (such as cherry tomatoes, cucumber slices, bell pepper strips, carrot sticks, celery sticks, olives, etc.)
- Optional: cheese slices, herbs, or other edible decorations for added details

Instructions:

1. Spread a thin layer of cream cheese or hummus onto each cracker to act as a base for the veggie faces.
2. Let your imagination run wild as you create different facial features using assorted vegetables! Here are some ideas to get you started:
    - Use cherry tomatoes or cucumber slices for eyes.
    - Use bell pepper strips or carrot sticks for smiles or eyebrows.
    - Use celery sticks or carrot sticks for noses.
    - Use olives or carrot rounds for pupils.
    - Get creative with other vegetables to create hair, hats, or accessories.
3. Arrange the vegetable pieces on top of the cream cheese or hummus on the crackers to create fun and colorful veggie faces.
4. If desired, add additional details using cheese slices, herbs, or other edible decorations.
5. Serve the Veggie Faces on Crackers as a fun and nutritious snack or appetizer for kids and adults alike!

These Veggie Faces on Crackers are not only visually appealing but also packed with vitamins, minerals, and fiber from the colorful assortment of vegetables. They're perfect for parties, playdates, or as a creative way to encourage picky eaters to try new vegetables. Let your imagination soar as you create your own veggie masterpieces!

Veggie Chips (Baked)

Ingredients:

- Assorted vegetables (such as sweet potatoes, carrots, beets, zucchini, or parsnips)
- Olive oil
- Salt and pepper, to taste
- Optional seasonings (such as garlic powder, paprika, or herbs)

Instructions:

1. Preheat your oven to 375°F (190°C). Line a baking sheet with parchment paper or a silicone baking mat.
2. Wash and peel the vegetables, if desired. Use a mandoline slicer or a sharp knife to thinly slice the vegetables into uniform rounds or chips.
3. In a large mixing bowl, toss the vegetable slices with a drizzle of olive oil, ensuring they are evenly coated.
4. Season the vegetable slices with salt, pepper, and any other desired seasonings, tossing to coat evenly.
5. Arrange the seasoned vegetable slices in a single layer on the prepared baking sheet, making sure they do not overlap.
6. Bake in the preheated oven for 15-20 minutes, flipping halfway through, or until the veggie chips are golden brown and crispy.
7. Keep an eye on them towards the end of the baking time to prevent burning.
8. Once baked, remove the veggie chips from the oven and let them cool on the baking sheet for a few minutes before serving.
9. Serve the baked veggie chips as a delicious and nutritious snack on their own or with your favorite dip.

These Baked Veggie Chips are not only crunchy and satisfying but also packed with vitamins, minerals, and fiber from the vegetables. Feel free to experiment with different vegetable varieties and seasonings to create your own custom flavors. Enjoy these guilt-free chips as a healthier alternative to traditional potato chips!

Chocolate Banana Sushi

Ingredients:

- 1 large banana, peeled
- 2-3 tablespoons chocolate hazelnut spread or melted chocolate
- 1/2 cup crispy rice cereal or crushed graham crackers
- Optional toppings: shredded coconut, chopped nuts, sprinkles, or mini chocolate chips

Instructions:

1. Lay a piece of plastic wrap or parchment paper on a clean surface.
2. Place the peeled banana on the plastic wrap or parchment paper horizontally.
3. Spread a thin layer of chocolate hazelnut spread or melted chocolate evenly over the top surface of the banana.
4. Sprinkle crispy rice cereal or crushed graham crackers evenly over the chocolate-covered banana, pressing gently to adhere.
5. Optionally, sprinkle additional toppings like shredded coconut, chopped nuts, sprinkles, or mini chocolate chips over the crispy rice cereal or crushed graham crackers.
6. Carefully roll the banana up in the plastic wrap or parchment paper, starting from one end and rolling tightly to form a sushi roll shape.
7. Once rolled, gently press the edges to seal.
8. Refrigerate the chocolate banana sushi roll for at least 30 minutes to allow it to firm up.
9. Remove the plastic wrap or parchment paper from the sushi roll and slice it into bite-sized pieces using a sharp knife.
10. Arrange the chocolate banana sushi pieces on a plate and serve immediately.

These Chocolate Banana Sushi rolls are not only delicious but also customizable. Feel free to get creative with different toppings and coatings to suit your taste preferences. Enjoy these sweet sushi treats as a fun dessert or snack!

Carrot and Hummus Snack Packs

Ingredients:

- Baby carrots or carrot sticks
- Hummus (store-bought or homemade)
- Optional: celery sticks, cucumber slices, bell pepper strips, or any other favorite raw vegetables for dipping

Instructions:

1. Wash and prepare the raw vegetables by cutting them into sticks, slices, or strips, depending on your preference.
2. Portion out individual servings of hummus into small containers with lids. You can use reusable containers or small disposable containers for convenience.
3. Place a handful of baby carrots or carrot sticks into small plastic bags or reusable snack bags. Alternatively, you can use small plastic containers or bento boxes.
4. If desired, add additional raw vegetables like celery sticks, cucumber slices, or bell pepper strips to the snack packs.
5. Seal the containers or bags tightly with lids or zipper closures to keep the vegetables and hummus fresh.
6. Pack the Carrot and Hummus Snack Packs in lunchboxes, backpacks, or coolers for easy access on the go.
7. When ready to eat, simply dip the raw vegetables into the hummus and enjoy!

These Carrot and Hummus Snack Packs are not only convenient but also packed with fiber, vitamins, and minerals from the raw vegetables and protein from the hummus. They make a great snack option for kids and adults alike, whether as a mid-morning pick-me-up, an afternoon snack, or a light pre-workout bite. Feel free to customize the snack packs with your favorite raw vegetables and hummus flavors for variety and enjoyment!

Crunchy Granola Bars

Ingredients:

- 2 cups old-fashioned oats
- 1/2 cup chopped nuts (such as almonds, pecans, or walnuts)
- 1/4 cup honey or maple syrup
- 1/4 cup peanut butter or almond butter
- 1/4 cup coconut oil or butter
- 1/4 cup packed brown sugar
- 1 teaspoon vanilla extract
- Pinch of salt
- Optional mix-ins: dried fruit (such as raisins, cranberries, or apricots), chocolate chips, coconut flakes, seeds (such as sunflower or pumpkin seeds)

Instructions:

1. Preheat your oven to 350°F (175°C). Line a 9x9-inch baking pan with parchment paper, leaving some overhang on the sides for easy removal later.
2. In a large mixing bowl, combine the oats and chopped nuts. Set aside.
3. In a small saucepan over medium heat, combine the honey or maple syrup, peanut butter or almond butter, coconut oil or butter, brown sugar, vanilla extract, and salt. Stir continuously until the mixture is smooth and well combined.
4. Pour the wet mixture over the dry ingredients in the mixing bowl. Stir until all the oats and nuts are evenly coated.
5. If using any optional mix-ins, fold them into the granola mixture at this point.
6. Transfer the granola mixture to the prepared baking pan. Use a spatula or the back of a spoon to press the mixture firmly and evenly into the pan.
7. Bake in the preheated oven for 20-25 minutes, or until the edges are golden brown and the granola bars are set.
8. Remove from the oven and let cool completely in the pan on a wire rack.
9. Once cooled, use the parchment paper overhang to lift the granola slab out of the pan. Place it on a cutting board and use a sharp knife to slice into bars or squares.
10. Store the Crunchy Granola Bars in an airtight container at room temperature for up to one week, or in the refrigerator for longer freshness.

These Crunchy Granola Bars are not only delicious but also customizable. Feel free to swap out the nuts, sweeteners, or mix-ins to suit your taste preferences. They're perfect for breakfast on the go, midday snacks, or as a wholesome treat anytime you need a little pick-me-up!

Mini Meatball Subs

Ingredients:

For the meatballs:

- 1 lb ground beef or turkey
- 1/2 cup breadcrumbs
- 1/4 cup grated Parmesan cheese
- 1 egg
- 2 cloves garlic, minced
- 1 teaspoon dried oregano
- 1 teaspoon dried basil
- Salt and pepper, to taste
- Olive oil, for cooking

For assembling:

- Mini sub rolls or dinner rolls, sliced in half
- Marinara sauce
- Shredded mozzarella cheese
- Chopped fresh parsley, for garnish (optional)

Instructions:

1. Preheat your oven to 375°F (190°C). Line a baking sheet with parchment paper or foil.
2. In a large mixing bowl, combine the ground beef or turkey, breadcrumbs, grated Parmesan cheese, egg, minced garlic, dried oregano, dried basil, salt, and pepper. Mix until well combined.
3. Shape the mixture into small meatballs, about 1 inch in diameter.
4. Heat a drizzle of olive oil in a large skillet over medium heat. Add the meatballs in batches and cook until browned on all sides, about 2-3 minutes per side. Transfer the browned meatballs to the prepared baking sheet.
5. Once all the meatballs are browned, transfer the baking sheet to the preheated oven and bake for 10-12 minutes, or until the meatballs are cooked through.

6. While the meatballs are baking, slice the mini sub rolls or dinner rolls in half and spread a spoonful of marinara sauce on the bottom half of each roll.
7. When the meatballs are done, remove them from the oven and place one meatball on each roll. Spoon a little more marinara sauce over each meatball.
8. Sprinkle shredded mozzarella cheese over the meatballs and sauce on each roll.
9. Return the assembled mini meatball subs to the oven and bake for an additional 5 minutes, or until the cheese is melted and bubbly.
10. Remove from the oven and sprinkle chopped fresh parsley over the subs for garnish, if desired.
11. Serve the Mini Meatball Subs warm, and enjoy!

These Mini Meatball Subs are sure to be a hit with family and friends. They're easy to make and packed with flavor, making them a crowd-pleasing option for any occasion!

Fruit and Yogurt Parfaits

Ingredients:

- Greek yogurt (plain or flavored)
- Fresh fruits (such as berries, sliced bananas, diced mangoes, or chopped kiwi)
- Granola or your favorite cereal
- Honey or maple syrup (optional, for extra sweetness)
- Nuts or seeds (such as almonds, walnuts, or pumpkin seeds) (optional, for added crunch)

Instructions:

1. Start by layering a spoonful of Greek yogurt at the bottom of a glass or bowl.
2. Add a layer of fresh fruits on top of the yogurt. You can use a single type of fruit or a combination of your favorites.
3. Sprinkle a layer of granola or cereal over the fruits. This adds crunch and texture to the parfait.
4. If desired, drizzle a little honey or maple syrup over the granola layer for extra sweetness.
5. Repeat the layers until the glass or bowl is filled, alternating between yogurt, fruits, and granola.
6. Finish the parfait with a final layer of Greek yogurt on top.
7. Optionally, garnish the parfait with additional fresh fruits, nuts, or seeds for extra flavor and presentation.
8. Serve the Fruit and Yogurt Parfaits immediately, or cover and refrigerate them for later enjoyment.

These Fruit and Yogurt Parfaits are not only delicious but also customizable. Feel free to experiment with different combinations of fruits, yogurt flavors, granola varieties, and toppings to suit your taste preferences. They're a great way to enjoy a healthy and satisfying snack or meal any time of the day!

Veggie Rainbow Wraps

Ingredients:

- Large whole grain or spinach tortillas
- Hummus or cream cheese (for spreading)
- Assorted vegetables, thinly sliced or julienned (such as red bell peppers, orange carrots, yellow bell peppers, green cucumbers, purple cabbage, and avocado)
- Optional add-ins: shredded lettuce, spinach leaves, alfalfa sprouts, or any other favorite vegetables
- Optional protein: sliced tofu, grilled chicken, or chickpeas

Instructions:

1. Lay a tortilla flat on a clean surface.
2. Spread a thin layer of hummus or cream cheese evenly over the entire surface of the tortilla.
3. Arrange the thinly sliced or julienned vegetables in rows across the center of the tortilla, creating a rainbow pattern. Start with the red vegetables (such as bell peppers), followed by orange (carrots), yellow (bell peppers), green (cucumbers), and purple (cabbage), leaving space at the bottom to fold.
4. Optionally, add any additional vegetables or protein of your choice on top of the rainbow rows.
5. If desired, drizzle a little extra hummus or dressing over the vegetables for added flavor.
6. Carefully fold the bottom edge of the tortilla up over the vegetables, then fold in the sides, and roll tightly to form a wrap.
7. Slice the Veggie Rainbow Wrap in half diagonally, if desired, and secure each half with toothpicks to hold them together.
8. Serve the Veggie Rainbow Wraps immediately, or wrap them tightly in plastic wrap or parchment paper for later enjoyment.

These Veggie Rainbow Wraps are not only visually appealing but also packed with vitamins, minerals, fiber, and other essential nutrients from the colorful assortment of vegetables. They make a great option for a healthy lunch, light dinner, or portable snack.

Feel free to customize the wraps with your favorite vegetables, spreads, and protein sources for endless flavor combinations!

Mini Corn Dog Muffins

Ingredients:

- 1 cup all-purpose flour
- 1 cup yellow cornmeal
- 1/4 cup granulated sugar
- 1 tablespoon baking powder
- 1/2 teaspoon salt
- 1 cup milk
- 2 large eggs
- 1/4 cup unsalted butter, melted
- 1 cup shredded cheddar cheese
- 8-10 hot dogs, cut into bite-sized pieces
- Optional: ketchup, mustard, or your favorite dipping sauce for serving

Instructions:

1. Preheat your oven to 400°F (200°C). Grease a mini muffin tin with cooking spray or line it with paper liners.
2. In a large mixing bowl, whisk together the flour, cornmeal, sugar, baking powder, and salt until well combined.
3. In a separate bowl, whisk together the milk, eggs, and melted butter until smooth.
4. Pour the wet ingredients into the dry ingredients and stir until just combined. Be careful not to overmix.
5. Fold in the shredded cheddar cheese until evenly distributed throughout the batter.
6. Fill each mini muffin cup halfway with the batter.
7. Place a piece of hot dog into the center of each muffin cup, pressing it down slightly into the batter.
8. Bake in the preheated oven for 12-15 minutes, or until the muffins are golden brown and a toothpick inserted into the center comes out clean.
9. Remove the mini corn dog muffins from the oven and let them cool in the muffin tin for a few minutes before transferring them to a wire rack to cool completely.
10. Serve the mini corn dog muffins warm with ketchup, mustard, or your favorite dipping sauce on the side.

These Mini Corn Dog Muffins are sure to be a hit with kids and adults alike. They're bite-sized, portable, and packed with savory flavor. Enjoy them as a fun party appetizer, after-school snack, or a quick and easy meal on busy days!

Cheesy Cauliflower Tots

Ingredients:

- 1 medium head cauliflower, chopped into florets
- 1/2 cup grated Parmesan cheese
- 1/2 cup shredded mozzarella cheese
- 1/4 cup breadcrumbs
- 1 egg
- 2 cloves garlic, minced
- 1 teaspoon dried oregano
- 1 teaspoon dried parsley
- 1/2 teaspoon salt
- 1/4 teaspoon black pepper
- Cooking spray or olive oil, for greasing

Instructions:

1. Preheat your oven to 400°F (200°C). Line a baking sheet with parchment paper or aluminum foil and lightly grease it with cooking spray or olive oil.
2. Steam the cauliflower florets until tender, about 5-7 minutes. Drain well and let cool slightly.
3. Once the cauliflower has cooled, place it in a clean kitchen towel or cheesecloth and squeeze out as much excess moisture as possible.
4. In a large mixing bowl, combine the cauliflower, grated Parmesan cheese, shredded mozzarella cheese, breadcrumbs, egg, minced garlic, dried oregano, dried parsley, salt, and black pepper. Mix until well combined.
5. Shape the cauliflower mixture into small tots or cylinders, about 1 inch in size, and place them on the prepared baking sheet.
6. Lightly spray the tops of the cauliflower tots with cooking spray or drizzle with olive oil.
7. Bake in the preheated oven for 20-25 minutes, or until the tots are golden brown and crispy on the outside.
8. Remove from the oven and let cool for a few minutes before serving.
9. Serve the Cheesy Cauliflower Tots warm as a delicious and nutritious snack or appetizer.

These Cheesy Cauliflower Tots are not only crispy and flavorful but also low in carbs and high in fiber, making them a guilt-free snack or side dish. Enjoy them on their own or with your favorite dipping sauce, such as marinara, ranch, or ketchup. They're sure to be a hit with both kids and adults!

Apple Chips (Baked)

Ingredients:

- 2 large apples (any variety you prefer)
- Cinnamon (optional)
- Sugar (optional)

Instructions:

1. Preheat your oven to 200°F (93°C). Line a baking sheet with parchment paper or a silicone baking mat.
2. Wash the apples thoroughly and pat them dry with a clean kitchen towel.
3. Using a sharp knife or a mandoline slicer, thinly slice the apples crosswise into rounds, about 1/8 inch thick. Try to make the slices as uniform as possible for even baking.
4. If desired, you can sprinkle the apple slices with a little cinnamon or sugar for added flavor. This step is optional, depending on your taste preferences.
5. Arrange the apple slices in a single layer on the prepared baking sheet, making sure they are not touching or overlapping.
6. Place the baking sheet in the preheated oven and bake the apple slices for 1.5 to 2 hours, or until they are dried out and crispy. The baking time may vary depending on the thickness of the slices and the moisture content of the apples.
7. After the first hour of baking, flip the apple slices over with a spatula to ensure even drying.
8. Keep an eye on the apple chips towards the end of the baking time to prevent burning. They should be crispy but not overly browned.
9. Once the apple chips are done baking, remove them from the oven and let them cool completely on the baking sheet.
10. Once cooled, transfer the apple chips to an airtight container or resealable bag for storage. They can be kept at room temperature for several days.

These baked apple chips are a delicious and healthy alternative to store-bought snacks.

They're naturally sweet, crispy, and perfect for munching on anytime you need a quick pick-me-up. Enjoy them as a standalone snack, or serve them alongside yogurt, cheese, or nut butter for a tasty and nutritious treat!

Cheesy Spinach Muffins

Ingredients:

- 2 cups all-purpose flour
- 1 tablespoon baking powder
- 1/2 teaspoon salt
- 1/4 teaspoon black pepper
- 2 cups fresh spinach, finely chopped
- 1 cup shredded cheddar cheese
- 1/4 cup grated Parmesan cheese
- 2 large eggs
- 1 cup milk
- 1/4 cup unsalted butter, melted
- 1/4 cup plain Greek yogurt or sour cream

Instructions:

1. Preheat your oven to 375°F (190°C). Grease a muffin tin or line it with paper liners.
2. In a large mixing bowl, whisk together the flour, baking powder, salt, and black pepper until well combined.
3. Add the finely chopped spinach, shredded cheddar cheese, and grated Parmesan cheese to the dry ingredients. Stir until the spinach and cheese are evenly distributed throughout the flour mixture.
4. In a separate bowl, beat the eggs until well blended. Stir in the milk, melted butter, and Greek yogurt or sour cream until smooth.
5. Pour the wet ingredients into the dry ingredients and gently fold them together until just combined. Be careful not to overmix; the batter should be slightly lumpy.
6. Spoon the batter into the prepared muffin tin, filling each cup about 3/4 full.
7. Optional: sprinkle a little extra shredded cheddar cheese on top of each muffin for added cheesiness.
8. Bake in the preheated oven for 18-20 minutes, or until the muffins are golden brown and a toothpick inserted into the center comes out clean.
9. Remove the muffin tin from the oven and let the muffins cool in the tin for a few minutes before transferring them to a wire rack to cool completely.
10. Serve the Cheesy Spinach Muffins warm or at room temperature. Enjoy!

These Cheesy Spinach Muffins are not only delicious but also packed with nutrients from the spinach and cheese. They're perfect for a quick breakfast on the go, a savory addition to brunch, or a satisfying snack any time of the day. Store any leftovers in an airtight container in the refrigerator and reheat them briefly in the microwave before serving. Enjoy!

Yogurt Bark with Berries and Granola

Ingredients:

- 2 cups Greek yogurt (plain or flavored)
- 1/4 cup honey or maple syrup
- 1 teaspoon vanilla extract
- 1 cup mixed berries (such as strawberries, blueberries, raspberries)
- 1/4 cup granola
- Optional: shredded coconut, chopped nuts, chocolate chips, dried fruit, or any other favorite toppings

Instructions:

1. Line a baking sheet with parchment paper or a silicone baking mat.
2. In a mixing bowl, combine the Greek yogurt, honey or maple syrup, and vanilla extract. Stir until smooth and well combined.
3. Spread the yogurt mixture evenly onto the prepared baking sheet, using a spatula to smooth it out into a thin layer.
4. Sprinkle the mixed berries evenly over the yogurt layer, pressing them gently into the yogurt.
5. Sprinkle the granola (and any other desired toppings) evenly over the berries, pressing lightly to adhere.
6. Optional: drizzle a little extra honey or maple syrup over the top for added sweetness.
7. Place the baking sheet in the freezer and freeze for at least 2-3 hours, or until the yogurt bark is completely frozen.
8. Once frozen, remove the baking sheet from the freezer and use a sharp knife to break the yogurt bark into pieces.
9. Serve the Yogurt Bark with Berries and Granola immediately as a refreshing snack or dessert.
10. Store any leftovers in an airtight container in the freezer for future enjoyment.

This Yogurt Bark with Berries and Granola is not only delicious but also packed with protein, vitamins, and minerals from the Greek yogurt and fresh berries. It's a perfect make-ahead snack or dessert that's sure to please both kids and adults alike. Feel free to customize the toppings to suit your taste preferences and dietary needs. Enjoy!

Cucumber and Cream Cheese Sandwiches

Ingredients:

- 8 slices of bread (white, whole wheat, or your favorite type)
- 1 large cucumber, thinly sliced
- 4 ounces (about 1/2 cup) cream cheese, softened
- 1-2 tablespoons fresh dill, chopped (optional)
- Salt and pepper, to taste

Instructions:

1. Trim the crusts off the bread slices, if desired, for a more elegant presentation. Alternatively, you can leave the crusts on for a heartier sandwich.
2. In a small bowl, mix the softened cream cheese with the chopped fresh dill, if using. Season with salt and pepper to taste.
3. Spread a thin layer of the cream cheese mixture onto one side of each bread slice.
4. Arrange the thinly sliced cucumber rounds evenly over the cream cheese layer on half of the bread slices.
5. Place the remaining bread slices on top of the cucumber slices to form sandwiches, with the cream cheese sides facing inward.
6. Gently press down on each sandwich to compact the filling slightly.
7. If desired, you can cut the sandwiches into quarters or triangles for serving.
8. Serve the Cucumber and Cream Cheese Sandwiches immediately, or cover them with plastic wrap and refrigerate until ready to serve.

These Cucumber and Cream Cheese Sandwiches are simple yet elegant, making them perfect for afternoon tea, brunch, picnics, or as a light lunch option. The combination of creamy cheese and crisp cucumber is wonderfully refreshing, especially on warm days. Feel free to customize the sandwiches by adding other ingredients like fresh herbs, lemon zest, or smoked salmon for added flavor. Enjoy!

Sweet Potato Fries (Baked)

Ingredients:

- 2 large sweet potatoes
- 2 tablespoons olive oil
- 1 teaspoon paprika
- 1/2 teaspoon garlic powder
- 1/2 teaspoon onion powder
- Salt and pepper to taste

Instructions:

1. Preheat your oven to 425°F (220°C). Line a baking sheet with parchment paper or aluminum foil.
2. Peel the sweet potatoes and cut them into uniform fries, about 1/4 to 1/2 inch thick.
3. Place the sweet potato fries in a large bowl. Drizzle with olive oil and sprinkle with paprika, garlic powder, onion powder, salt, and pepper. Toss until the fries are evenly coated with the seasoning.
4. Arrange the seasoned sweet potato fries in a single layer on the prepared baking sheet, making sure they are not overlapping.
5. Bake in the preheated oven for 20-25 minutes, flipping halfway through, or until the fries are crispy and golden brown on the outside and tender on the inside.
6. Remove from the oven and let cool for a few minutes before serving.
7. Serve the baked sweet potato fries hot with your favorite dipping sauce, such as ketchup, aioli, or sriracha mayo.

These baked sweet potato fries are delicious, crispy, and packed with flavor. They make a great side dish or snack, and they're perfect for dipping into your favorite sauces. Enjoy!

Veggie Stuffed Bell Peppers

Ingredients:

- 4 large bell peppers (any color)
- 1 cup cooked quinoa or rice
- 1 can (15 oz) black beans, drained and rinsed
- 1 cup corn kernels (fresh, frozen, or canned)
- 1 cup diced tomatoes (fresh or canned)
- 1/2 cup diced onion
- 2 cloves garlic, minced
- 1 teaspoon ground cumin
- 1 teaspoon chili powder
- 1/2 teaspoon paprika
- Salt and pepper, to taste
- 1 cup shredded cheese (cheddar, mozzarella, or your favorite)

Instructions:

1. Preheat your oven to 375°F (190°C). Grease a baking dish large enough to hold the bell peppers.
2. Cut the tops off the bell peppers and remove the seeds and membranes from inside. Set aside.
3. In a large mixing bowl, combine the cooked quinoa or rice, black beans, corn kernels, diced tomatoes, diced onion, minced garlic, ground cumin, chili powder, paprika, salt, and pepper. Stir until well combined.
4. Stuff each bell pepper with the quinoa mixture, pressing down gently to pack it in. You may have some mixture leftover, depending on the size of your bell peppers.
5. Place the stuffed bell peppers upright in the prepared baking dish.
6. Cover the baking dish with foil and bake in the preheated oven for 25-30 minutes, or until the peppers are tender.
7. Remove the foil from the baking dish and sprinkle the shredded cheese evenly over the tops of the stuffed peppers.
8. Return the baking dish to the oven and bake for an additional 5-10 minutes, or until the cheese is melted and bubbly.
9. Remove from the oven and let the stuffed bell peppers cool for a few minutes before serving.

10. Serve the Veggie Stuffed Bell Peppers hot, garnished with chopped fresh cilantro or parsley, if desired.

These Veggie Stuffed Bell Peppers are hearty, flavorful, and packed with protein and fiber from the quinoa, black beans, and vegetables. They make a satisfying main dish for vegetarians and meat-lovers alike. Enjoy them for dinner, and leftovers can be enjoyed for lunch the next day!

Homemade Applesauce

Ingredients:

- 6-8 medium-sized apples (any variety you prefer)
- 1/2 cup water
- 2-3 tablespoons granulated sugar (optional, adjust to taste)
- 1 teaspoon ground cinnamon (optional)

Instructions:

1. Peel, core, and chop the apples into small chunks. You can leave the peel on for added fiber and nutrients if you prefer.
2. Place the chopped apples in a large saucepan or pot. Add the water to the pot.
3. Optional: Stir in the granulated sugar and ground cinnamon, if using, for added sweetness and flavor.
4. Cover the pot and bring the apples and water to a boil over medium-high heat.
5. Once boiling, reduce the heat to low and let the apples simmer, covered, for 15-20 minutes, or until they are soft and easily mashable with a fork.
6. Remove the pot from the heat and let the cooked apples cool slightly.
7. Using a potato masher or immersion blender, mash or blend the cooked apples until you reach your desired consistency. For smoother applesauce, blend it longer; for chunkier applesauce, mash it less.
8. Taste the applesauce and adjust the sweetness and seasoning if needed, adding more sugar or cinnamon to taste.
9. Once you're happy with the flavor and texture, transfer the homemade applesauce to airtight containers or jars for storage.
10. Allow the applesauce to cool completely before sealing the containers and storing them in the refrigerator.
11. Homemade applesauce can be stored in the refrigerator for up to 1 week.

Enjoy your homemade applesauce as a healthy snack, dessert, or accompaniment to savory dishes. It's delicious served warm or chilled, and you can also use it as a topping for oatmeal, pancakes, yogurt, or ice cream. Feel free to experiment with different apple varieties and spice combinations to create your own unique flavors!

Mini Chicken Tacos

Ingredients:

- 1 lb boneless, skinless chicken breasts, diced into small pieces
- 1 tablespoon olive oil
- 1 teaspoon chili powder
- 1/2 teaspoon ground cumin
- 1/2 teaspoon garlic powder
- Salt and pepper, to taste
- Mini tortillas (corn or flour)
- Toppings: shredded lettuce, diced tomatoes, shredded cheese, sour cream, salsa, guacamole, etc.

Instructions:

1. In a large skillet, heat the olive oil over medium heat.
2. Add the diced chicken to the skillet and season with chili powder, cumin, garlic powder, salt, and pepper. Cook, stirring occasionally, until the chicken is cooked through and no longer pink, about 8-10 minutes.
3. While the chicken is cooking, warm the mini tortillas according to package instructions.
4. Once the chicken is cooked, remove it from the heat and set it aside.
5. To assemble the mini tacos, place a spoonful of the cooked chicken onto each mini tortilla.
6. Top each taco with your choice of toppings, such as shredded lettuce, diced tomatoes, shredded cheese, sour cream, salsa, or guacamole.
7. Serve the mini chicken tacos immediately, and enjoy!

These mini chicken tacos are customizable, so feel free to get creative with the toppings and seasonings. You can also make them ahead of time and reheat them in the oven or microwave before serving. They're sure to be a hit with family and friends at your next gathering!

Zucchini Pizza Bites

Ingredients:

- 2 medium zucchinis
- 1/2 cup marinara sauce
- 1 cup shredded mozzarella cheese
- Your favorite pizza toppings (pepperoni slices, diced bell peppers, sliced olives, etc.)
- Olive oil
- Salt and pepper, to taste
- Optional: grated Parmesan cheese, chopped fresh basil, red pepper flakes

Instructions:

1. Preheat your oven to 400°F (200°C). Line a baking sheet with parchment paper or aluminum foil.
2. Slice the zucchinis into 1/4-inch thick rounds. Place the zucchini rounds on the prepared baking sheet in a single layer.
3. Lightly brush the tops of the zucchini rounds with olive oil and season with salt and pepper.
4. Spoon a small amount of marinara sauce onto each zucchini round, spreading it out evenly.
5. Sprinkle shredded mozzarella cheese over the marinara sauce on each zucchini round.
6. Top each zucchini round with your favorite pizza toppings, such as pepperoni slices, diced bell peppers, or sliced olives.
7. Optional: sprinkle grated Parmesan cheese, chopped fresh basil, or red pepper flakes over the top of the pizza bites for extra flavor.
8. Bake in the preheated oven for 12-15 minutes, or until the cheese is melted and bubbly and the zucchini is tender.
9. Remove from the oven and let the zucchini pizza bites cool for a few minutes before serving.
10. Serve the zucchini pizza bites warm as a delicious and nutritious appetizer or snack.

These zucchini pizza bites are a great way to enjoy the flavors of pizza in a healthier way. They're low-carb, gluten-free, and packed with vitamins and minerals from the zucchini. Plus, they're customizable, so you can add your favorite pizza toppings to suit your taste preferences. Enjoy!

Cheese and Veggie Quesadilla Dippers

Ingredients:

- 4 large flour tortillas
- 1 cup shredded cheese (cheddar, mozzarella, or your favorite)
- 1/2 cup diced bell peppers (any color)
- 1/2 cup diced tomatoes
- 1/4 cup sliced black olives
- 1/4 cup chopped green onions
- Olive oil or cooking spray
- Salsa, sour cream, or guacamole for dipping (optional)

Instructions:

1. Preheat your oven to 375°F (190°C). Line a baking sheet with parchment paper.
2. Place one tortilla on a flat surface. Sprinkle a quarter of the shredded cheese evenly over half of the tortilla.
3. Add a quarter of the diced bell peppers, diced tomatoes, sliced black olives, and chopped green onions on top of the cheese.
4. Fold the tortilla in half to cover the filling, creating a half-moon shape.
5. Repeat the process with the remaining tortillas and filling ingredients.
6. Lightly brush or spray both sides of each quesadilla with olive oil or cooking spray.
7. Place the quesadillas on the prepared baking sheet and bake in the preheated oven for 10-12 minutes, or until the tortillas are crispy and golden brown and the cheese is melted.
8. Remove from the oven and let the quesadillas cool for a few minutes before slicing them into wedges or strips.
9. Serve the cheese and veggie quesadilla dippers warm with salsa, sour cream, or guacamole for dipping, if desired.

These cheese and veggie quesadilla dippers are versatile and customizable, so feel free to add or substitute your favorite vegetables or cheese. They're perfect for serving as a snack, appetizer, or even a light meal. Enjoy!

Trail Mix Energy Bites

Ingredients:

- 1 cup rolled oats
- 1/2 cup nut butter (peanut butter, almond butter, etc.)
- 1/4 cup honey or maple syrup
- 1/4 cup mini chocolate chips
- 1/4 cup chopped nuts (such as almonds, walnuts, or cashews)
- 1/4 cup dried fruit (such as raisins, cranberries, or chopped apricots)
- 1/4 cup shredded coconut (optional)
- 1 teaspoon vanilla extract
- Pinch of salt

Instructions:

1. In a large mixing bowl, combine the rolled oats, nut butter, honey or maple syrup, mini chocolate chips, chopped nuts, dried fruit, shredded coconut (if using), vanilla extract, and a pinch of salt.
2. Stir until all the ingredients are well combined and the mixture starts to come together.
3. If the mixture seems too dry, you can add a little more nut butter or honey/maple syrup to help bind it together.
4. Once the mixture is well combined and holds together when pressed, use your hands to roll it into small balls, about 1 inch in diameter.
5. Place the energy bites on a baking sheet lined with parchment paper or wax paper.
6. Refrigerate the energy bites for at least 30 minutes to help them firm up.
7. Once chilled, the energy bites can be stored in an airtight container in the refrigerator for up to two weeks.
8. Enjoy the trail mix energy bites as a quick and portable snack whenever you need a boost of energy!

These trail mix energy bites are customizable, so feel free to experiment with different ingredients based on your preferences and dietary restrictions. They're perfect for on-the-go snacking, post-workout fuel, or satisfying a sweet craving in a healthier way. Enjoy!

Watermelon Popsicles

Ingredients:

- 4 cups diced seedless watermelon
- 1 tablespoon lime juice (optional)
- Sweetener of your choice (optional, depending on the sweetness of the watermelon)
- Popsicle molds
- Popsicle sticks

Instructions:

1. Place the diced watermelon in a blender or food processor. If desired, add lime juice for a tangy flavor.
2. Blend the watermelon until smooth. Taste the mixture and add sweetener if needed, depending on the sweetness of the watermelon.
3. Pour the watermelon mixture into popsicle molds, leaving a little space at the top for expansion.
4. Insert popsicle sticks into the molds.
5. Place the popsicle molds in the freezer and freeze for at least 4-6 hours, or until the popsicles are completely frozen.
6. Once frozen, remove the popsicle molds from the freezer.
7. To release the popsicles from the molds, run warm water over the outside of the molds for a few seconds until the popsicles loosen.
8. Serve the watermelon popsicles immediately and enjoy!

These watermelon popsicles are naturally sweet and refreshing, making them the perfect treat for hot summer days. You can also customize them by adding other fruits like strawberries, kiwi, or mint leaves for extra flavor. Enjoy these icy delights as a healthy and hydrating snack or dessert!

Turkey and Cheese Roll-Ups

Ingredients:

- Thinly sliced deli turkey
- Sliced cheese (cheddar, Swiss, provolone, etc.)
- Optional: mustard, mayonnaise, lettuce, tomato slices, pickle spears, etc.

Instructions:

1. Lay out a slice of deli turkey on a clean surface.
2. Place a slice of cheese on top of the turkey.
3. If desired, add a thin layer of mustard or mayonnaise on top of the cheese.
4. Add any additional toppings you like, such as lettuce, tomato slices, or pickle spears.
5. Starting at one end, roll up the turkey and cheese tightly into a cylinder shape.
6. Repeat with the remaining turkey slices and cheese slices.
7. Once all the roll-ups are assembled, you can serve them immediately or refrigerate them for later.

These turkey and cheese roll-ups are versatile and customizable, so feel free to experiment with different cheese varieties and toppings. They're perfect for packing in lunchboxes, serving as a party appetizer, or enjoying as a quick and easy snack any time of day. Enjoy!

Rainbow Veggie Skewers with Dip

Ingredients:

- Cherry tomatoes
- Red bell peppers, cut into chunks
- Orange bell peppers, cut into chunks
- Yellow bell peppers, cut into chunks
- Green bell peppers, cut into chunks
- Purple or blue potatoes, boiled and cut into chunks
- Red cabbage, thinly sliced
- Wooden or metal skewers
- Hummus or your favorite dip

Instructions:

1. Prepare the vegetables by washing and cutting them into bite-sized pieces.
2. Thread the vegetables onto the skewers in rainbow order, starting with the cherry tomatoes, followed by the red, orange, yellow, and green bell peppers, purple potatoes, and finally the red cabbage.
3. Repeat with the remaining skewers until all the vegetables are used up.
4. Arrange the rainbow veggie skewers on a platter or serving tray.
5. Serve the skewers with hummus or your favorite dip on the side for dipping.

These rainbow veggie skewers are not only visually appealing but also packed with vitamins, minerals, and fiber. They're a fun and nutritious way to enjoy a variety of colorful vegetables. Serve them at parties, picnics, or as a healthy snack for kids and adults alike. Enjoy!

Veggie Sushi Rolls

Ingredients:

- Sushi rice (prepared according to package instructions)
- Nori seaweed sheets
- Assorted vegetables, thinly sliced (such as cucumber, avocado, carrot, bell pepper, or lettuce)
- Optional: sesame seeds, tofu, pickled ginger, wasabi, soy sauce for serving

Instructions:

1. Lay a nori seaweed sheet on a bamboo sushi mat or a clean kitchen towel.
2. Spread a thin layer of prepared sushi rice evenly over the nori sheet, leaving about a 1-inch border at the top edge.
3. Arrange your choice of thinly sliced vegetables or other fillings in a horizontal line across the center of the rice.
4. Starting from the bottom edge, tightly roll the nori sheet over the fillings, using the sushi mat or towel to help shape the roll.
5. Continue rolling until you reach the top edge, then moisten the top edge with a little water to seal the roll.
6. Using a sharp knife, slice the sushi roll into individual pieces, about 1 inch thick.
7. Repeat the process with the remaining nori sheets, rice, and fillings.
8. Arrange the veggie sushi rolls on a serving platter and sprinkle with sesame seeds if desired.
9. Serve the veggie sushi rolls with pickled ginger, wasabi, and soy sauce for dipping.

These veggie sushi rolls are customizable, so feel free to experiment with different vegetable combinations and fillings to suit your taste preferences. They're perfect for serving as a healthy snack, appetizer, or light meal. Enjoy!

Mini Cheeseburger Sliders

Ingredients:

- 1 lb ground beef
- Salt and pepper, to taste
- 12 slider buns
- 6 slices of cheese (cheddar, American, Swiss, etc.), cut into quarters
- Optional toppings: lettuce, tomato slices, pickles, onions, ketchup, mustard, mayonnaise, etc.

Instructions:

1. Preheat your grill or skillet over medium-high heat.
2. Divide the ground beef into 12 equal portions and shape them into small patties, slightly larger than the size of the slider buns. Season each patty with salt and pepper.
3. Place the patties on the grill or skillet and cook for 2-3 minutes per side, or until they reach your desired level of doneness.
4. During the last minute of cooking, place a quarter slice of cheese on top of each patty to melt.
5. While the patties are cooking, split the slider buns in half and lightly toast them on the grill or skillet.
6. Once the patties are cooked and the cheese is melted, assemble the mini cheeseburger sliders by placing each patty on the bottom half of a slider bun.
7. Top each patty with your choice of optional toppings, such as lettuce, tomato slices, pickles, onions, ketchup, mustard, or mayonnaise.
8. Place the top half of the slider bun on top of the toppings to complete the sliders.
9. Secure each slider with a toothpick to hold it together.
10. Serve the mini cheeseburger sliders immediately, and enjoy!

These mini cheeseburger sliders are sure to be a hit with guests of all ages. They're customizable, so feel free to add your favorite toppings to suit your taste preferences. Enjoy them as a tasty appetizer, snack, or even a main course at your next gathering!

Fruit Salad with Honey Lime Dressing

Ingredients:

- Assorted fruits of your choice, such as strawberries, blueberries, raspberries, blackberries, pineapple, mango, kiwi, grapes, oranges, etc. (use a combination of colors and textures for the best presentation)
- 2 tablespoons honey
- 1 tablespoon freshly squeezed lime juice
- Zest of 1 lime
- Optional: fresh mint leaves for garnish

Instructions:

1. Wash and prepare the fruits as needed. Cut larger fruits into bite-sized pieces and leave smaller fruits whole.
2. Place the prepared fruits in a large mixing bowl.
3. In a small bowl, whisk together the honey, lime juice, and lime zest until well combined.
4. Pour the honey lime dressing over the fruits in the mixing bowl.
5. Gently toss the fruits with the dressing until they are evenly coated.
6. Taste the fruit salad and adjust the sweetness or tartness by adding more honey or lime juice if needed.
7. Optional: garnish the fruit salad with fresh mint leaves for extra flavor and presentation.
8. Serve the fruit salad immediately, or cover and refrigerate it until ready to serve.

This fruit salad with honey lime dressing is bursting with fresh, vibrant flavors. The honey lime dressing adds a subtle sweetness and tanginess that enhances the natural sweetness of the fruits. It's a light and refreshing dessert or side dish that's sure to be a hit at any gathering. Enjoy!

Veggie and Cheese Stuffed Breadsticks

Ingredients:

- 1 pound pizza dough (homemade or store-bought)
- 1 cup shredded mozzarella cheese
- 1/2 cup finely chopped assorted vegetables (such as bell peppers, onions, mushrooms, spinach, etc.)
- 2 tablespoons grated Parmesan cheese
- 1 teaspoon garlic powder
- 1/2 teaspoon dried oregano
- 1/4 teaspoon salt
- Olive oil, for brushing
- Marinara sauce, for dipping (optional)

Instructions:

1. Preheat your oven to 400°F (200°C). Line a baking sheet with parchment paper or lightly grease it with cooking spray.
2. On a lightly floured surface, roll out the pizza dough into a large rectangle, about 1/4 inch thick.
3. Sprinkle the shredded mozzarella cheese evenly over the surface of the dough, leaving a small border around the edges.
4. Scatter the finely chopped vegetables over the cheese.
5. Starting from one long edge, tightly roll up the dough into a log, enclosing the cheese and vegetables inside.
6. Use a sharp knife to slice the dough log into 1-inch thick rounds.
7. Place the sliced rounds on the prepared baking sheet, leaving a little space between each one.
8. In a small bowl, mix together the grated Parmesan cheese, garlic powder, dried oregano, and salt.
9. Brush the tops of the breadsticks with olive oil, then sprinkle the Parmesan cheese mixture evenly over the tops.
10. Bake in the preheated oven for 15-20 minutes, or until the breadsticks are golden brown and cooked through.
11. Remove from the oven and let cool slightly before serving.

12. Serve the veggie and cheese stuffed breadsticks warm, with marinara sauce for dipping if desired.

These veggie and cheese stuffed breadsticks are savory, cheesy, and packed with flavor. They make a delicious appetizer or snack for any occasion, and they're sure to be a hit with family and friends. Enjoy!

Frozen Yogurt Bites with Fruit

Ingredients:

- 1 cup Greek yogurt (plain or flavored)
- 1 cup mixed fruit (such as berries, diced mango, kiwi, etc.)
- Optional: honey or maple syrup for added sweetness

Instructions:

1. Line a baking sheet with parchment paper or a silicone baking mat.
2. If desired, you can sweeten the Greek yogurt by stirring in a little honey or maple syrup.
3. Spoon small dollops of Greek yogurt onto the prepared baking sheet, leaving a little space between each one.
4. Press a piece of fruit into the center of each yogurt dollop.
5. Repeat the process until all the yogurt and fruit are used up.
6. Place the baking sheet in the freezer and freeze the yogurt bites for at least 2-3 hours, or until they are completely frozen.
7. Once frozen, remove the yogurt bites from the baking sheet and transfer them to an airtight container or freezer bag for storage.
8. Store the frozen yogurt bites in the freezer until ready to serve.
9. Serve the frozen yogurt bites straight from the freezer as a refreshing snack or dessert.

These frozen yogurt bites with fruit are not only delicious but also packed with protein, vitamins, and minerals from the Greek yogurt and fresh fruit. They're perfect for satisfying sweet cravings in a healthier way, and they're customizable too – feel free to mix and match different fruits to create your own unique flavor combinations. Enjoy!

Banana Oatmeal Cookies

Ingredients:

- 2 ripe bananas, mashed
- 1 cup rolled oats
- 1/4 cup peanut butter or almond butter
- 1/4 cup honey or maple syrup
- 1/4 cup raisins, chocolate chips, chopped nuts, or your favorite mix-ins (optional)
- 1/2 teaspoon ground cinnamon
- 1/2 teaspoon vanilla extract
- Pinch of salt

Instructions:

1. Preheat your oven to 350°F (175°C). Line a baking sheet with parchment paper or lightly grease it with cooking spray.
2. In a mixing bowl, combine the mashed bananas, rolled oats, peanut butter or almond butter, honey or maple syrup, mix-ins (if using), ground cinnamon, vanilla extract, and a pinch of salt. Stir until all the ingredients are well combined.
3. Drop spoonfuls of the cookie dough onto the prepared baking sheet, spacing them a few inches apart.
4. Use the back of a spoon or your fingers to flatten each cookie slightly.
5. Bake in the preheated oven for 12-15 minutes, or until the cookies are golden brown around the edges.
6. Remove from the oven and let the cookies cool on the baking sheet for a few minutes before transferring them to a wire rack to cool completely.
7. Once cooled, store the banana oatmeal cookies in an airtight container at room temperature for up to 3 days, or refrigerate them for longer storage.

These banana oatmeal cookies are soft, chewy, and naturally sweetened by the bananas and honey or maple syrup. They're perfect for breakfast, snack, or dessert, and they're great for using up overripe bananas. Feel free to customize them by adding your favorite mix-ins, such as raisins, chocolate chips, or chopped nuts. Enjoy!

Turkey and Veggie Pita Pockets

Ingredients:

- 4 whole wheat pita pockets
- 8 slices of deli turkey
- 1 cup mixed vegetables, thinly sliced or chopped (such as bell peppers, cucumber, tomato, lettuce, red onion, etc.)
- 1/2 cup hummus or tzatziki sauce
- Optional: crumbled feta cheese, olives, fresh herbs (such as parsley or mint), hot sauce, etc.

Instructions:

1. Warm the pita pockets in a toaster oven or microwave for a few seconds to make them more pliable.
2. Carefully cut open each pita pocket to create a pocket for the filling.
3. Spread a generous spoonful of hummus or tzatziki sauce inside each pita pocket.
4. Stuff each pita pocket with 2 slices of deli turkey and a handful of mixed vegetables.
5. If desired, sprinkle crumbled feta cheese over the filling and add any additional toppings, such as olives or fresh herbs.
6. Serve the turkey and veggie pita pockets immediately, or wrap them in foil or plastic wrap for a portable lunch option.

These turkey and veggie pita pockets are versatile and customizable, so feel free to use your favorite vegetables and sauces to suit your taste preferences. They're a great way to pack in protein, fiber, and vitamins, making them a healthy and satisfying meal option. Enjoy!

Veggie Chips and Salsa

Ingredients:

For the veggie chips:

- Assorted vegetables, such as sweet potatoes, beets, carrots, zucchini, or kale
- Olive oil
- Salt and pepper

For the salsa:

- 4 ripe tomatoes, diced
- 1/2 red onion, finely chopped
- 1 jalapeño pepper, seeded and finely chopped (optional, adjust to taste)
- 1/4 cup fresh cilantro, chopped
- Juice of 1 lime
- Salt and pepper, to taste

Instructions:

1. Preheat your oven to 375°F (190°C). Line a baking sheet with parchment paper.
2. Wash and peel the vegetables, if necessary. Slice them thinly into chips using a mandoline slicer or a sharp knife.
3. In a large mixing bowl, toss the sliced vegetables with a drizzle of olive oil, salt, and pepper until they are evenly coated.
4. Arrange the vegetable slices in a single layer on the prepared baking sheet.
5. Bake in the preheated oven for 10-15 minutes, or until the chips are golden brown and crispy. Keep an eye on them as cooking times may vary depending on the thickness of the slices and the type of vegetable.
6. While the veggie chips are baking, prepare the salsa. In a medium mixing bowl, combine the diced tomatoes, chopped red onion, jalapeño pepper (if using), chopped cilantro, lime juice, salt, and pepper. Stir until well combined.
7. Once the veggie chips are done baking, remove them from the oven and let them cool for a few minutes before serving.
8. Serve the veggie chips with the salsa on the side for dipping.

These homemade veggie chips and salsa are healthier alternatives to store-bought chips and salsa, as they are made with fresh, wholesome ingredients. They're perfect for snacking on while watching TV, entertaining guests, or taking on picnics. Enjoy!

Homemade Fruit Leather

Ingredients:

- 4 cups chopped fresh fruit (such as strawberries, peaches, apples, mangoes, etc.)
- 2-3 tablespoons honey or maple syrup (optional, depending on the sweetness of the fruit)
- 1 tablespoon lemon juice (optional, for added flavor and to prevent browning)
- Optional flavorings: vanilla extract, cinnamon, ginger, etc.

Instructions:

1. Preheat your oven to the lowest temperature setting (usually around 140°F or 60°C). If your oven doesn't go that low, use the lowest setting available.
2. Line a baking sheet with parchment paper or a silicone baking mat.
3. Place the chopped fruit in a blender or food processor and blend until smooth. If desired, you can strain the puree to remove any seeds or pulp, but it's not necessary.
4. Taste the fruit puree and add honey or maple syrup, if needed, to sweeten it. You can also add lemon juice for a tart flavor and to prevent browning.
5. Optional: stir in any additional flavorings, such as vanilla extract, cinnamon, or ginger, to enhance the flavor of the fruit leather.
6. Pour the fruit puree onto the prepared baking sheet and spread it out evenly with a spatula, making sure it's about 1/8 inch thick.
7. Place the baking sheet in the preheated oven and bake the fruit puree for 4-6 hours, or until it is no longer sticky to the touch and feels dry.
8. Remove the fruit leather from the oven and let it cool completely on the baking sheet.
9. Once cooled, use kitchen scissors or a sharp knife to cut the fruit leather into strips or squares.
10. Roll up the fruit leather strips or stack the squares and store them in an airtight container at room temperature for up to 1 week.

Homemade fruit leather is a great way to enjoy the natural sweetness of fresh fruit without any added sugars or preservatives. It's perfect for packing in lunchboxes, taking on hikes or road trips, or enjoying as a healthy snack any time of day. Feel free to experiment with different fruit combinations and flavorings to create your own unique fruit leather recipes. Enjoy!

English Muffin Pizzas

Ingredients:

- English muffins, split in half
- Tomato sauce or pizza sauce
- Shredded mozzarella cheese
- Your favorite pizza toppings (such as pepperoni slices, sliced bell peppers, sliced mushrooms, olives, etc.)
- Optional: dried oregano, dried basil, red pepper flakes

Instructions:

1. Preheat your oven to 375°F (190°C).
2. Place the English muffin halves on a baking sheet lined with parchment paper or aluminum foil, cut side up.
3. Spread a spoonful of tomato sauce or pizza sauce over each English muffin half, covering the surface evenly.
4. Sprinkle shredded mozzarella cheese over the sauce on each English muffin half.
5. Add your favorite pizza toppings on top of the cheese. Feel free to get creative and mix and match toppings to your liking.
6. Optional: sprinkle a pinch of dried oregano, dried basil, or red pepper flakes over the top of each English muffin pizza for extra flavor.
7. Place the baking sheet in the preheated oven and bake the English muffin pizzas for 10-12 minutes, or until the cheese is melted and bubbly and the edges of the muffins are lightly toasted.
8. Remove the English muffin pizzas from the oven and let them cool for a few minutes before serving.
9. Serve the English muffin pizzas warm as a quick and delicious meal or snack.

These English muffin pizzas are versatile and customizable, so feel free to experiment with different sauce, cheese, and topping combinations to suit your taste preferences. They're perfect for serving at parties, game days, or for a fun family dinner. Enjoy!

Veggie and Ham Breakfast Muffins

Ingredients:

- 6 large eggs
- 1/4 cup milk
- Salt and pepper, to taste
- 1 cup diced cooked ham
- 1/2 cup diced vegetables (such as bell peppers, onions, spinach, tomatoes, etc.)
- 1/2 cup shredded cheese (such as cheddar, mozzarella, or Swiss)
- Cooking spray or muffin liners

Instructions:

1. Preheat your oven to 375°F (190°C). Grease a muffin tin with cooking spray or line it with muffin liners.
2. In a large mixing bowl, whisk together the eggs and milk until well combined. Season with salt and pepper to taste.
3. Stir in the diced ham, diced vegetables, and shredded cheese until evenly distributed.
4. Pour the egg mixture into the prepared muffin tin, filling each muffin cup about three-quarters full.
5. Bake in the preheated oven for 20-25 minutes, or until the muffins are set in the center and lightly golden on top.
6. Remove the muffins from the oven and let them cool in the muffin tin for a few minutes before transferring them to a wire rack to cool completely.
7. Once cooled, store the veggie and ham breakfast muffins in an airtight container in the refrigerator for up to 3 days.
8. To reheat, simply microwave the muffins for 20-30 seconds until warmed through, or enjoy them cold.

These veggie and ham breakfast muffins are perfect for meal prep. You can make a batch ahead of time and store them in the refrigerator for a quick and easy breakfast on busy mornings. They're portable, filling, and packed with protein and vegetables to keep you satisfied until lunchtime. Enjoy!

Chicken and Veggie Stir-Fry

Ingredients:

- 2 boneless, skinless chicken breasts, thinly sliced
- 2 tablespoons soy sauce
- 1 tablespoon rice vinegar
- 1 tablespoon honey or brown sugar
- 2 cloves garlic, minced
- 1 teaspoon grated ginger
- 2 tablespoons vegetable oil
- 1 onion, thinly sliced
- 2 bell peppers, thinly sliced (any color)
- 1 cup broccoli florets
- 1 cup sliced mushrooms
- Optional garnishes: sliced green onions, sesame seeds

Instructions:

1. In a small bowl, mix together the soy sauce, rice vinegar, honey or brown sugar, minced garlic, and grated ginger to make the sauce. Set aside.
2. Heat one tablespoon of vegetable oil in a large skillet or wok over medium-high heat.
3. Add the sliced chicken breasts to the skillet and cook until they are no longer pink, about 4-5 minutes. Remove the cooked chicken from the skillet and set aside.
4. In the same skillet, add the remaining tablespoon of vegetable oil.
5. Add the sliced onion, bell peppers, broccoli florets, and sliced mushrooms to the skillet. Stir-fry the vegetables until they are crisp-tender, about 5-6 minutes.
6. Return the cooked chicken to the skillet with the vegetables.
7. Pour the sauce over the chicken and vegetables in the skillet. Stir well to coat everything evenly in the sauce.
8. Cook for an additional 1-2 minutes, or until the sauce has thickened slightly and everything is heated through.
9. Remove the skillet from the heat and garnish the chicken and veggie stir-fry with sliced green onions and sesame seeds, if desired.
10. Serve the stir-fry hot over cooked rice or noodles.

This chicken and veggie stir-fry is a versatile dish, so feel free to customize it with your favorite vegetables or protein sources. It's perfect for a quick weeknight dinner and can be easily adapted to suit your taste preferences. Enjoy!

Cheesy Zucchini Fritters

Ingredients:

- 2 medium zucchinis, grated
- 1 teaspoon salt
- 1/2 cup shredded cheddar cheese
- 1/4 cup grated Parmesan cheese
- 2 cloves garlic, minced
- 2 green onions, finely chopped
- 1/4 cup all-purpose flour
- 2 large eggs, lightly beaten
- 2 tablespoons olive oil, for frying
- Optional: sour cream or Greek yogurt for serving

Instructions:

1. Place the grated zucchini in a colander set over a bowl. Sprinkle with salt and let it sit for about 10 minutes to release excess moisture.
2. After 10 minutes, use your hands or a clean kitchen towel to squeeze out as much liquid from the zucchini as possible.
3. In a large mixing bowl, combine the grated zucchini, shredded cheddar cheese, grated Parmesan cheese, minced garlic, chopped green onions, all-purpose flour, and beaten eggs. Stir until all the ingredients are well combined.
4. Heat the olive oil in a large skillet over medium heat.
5. Once the oil is hot, spoon about 1/4 cup of the zucchini mixture into the skillet for each fritter, flattening it slightly with the back of the spoon.
6. Cook the fritters for 3-4 minutes on each side, or until they are golden brown and crispy.
7. Remove the cooked fritters from the skillet and place them on a plate lined with paper towels to drain any excess oil.
8. Repeat the process with the remaining zucchini mixture, adding more oil to the skillet as needed.
9. Serve the cheesy zucchini fritters hot, with sour cream or Greek yogurt for dipping if desired.

These cheesy zucchini fritters are crispy on the outside and tender on the inside, with a delicious cheesy flavor that's sure to please. They make a great appetizer, snack, or even a light meal when served with a salad on the side. Enjoy!

www.ingramcontent.com/pod-product-compliance
Lightning Source LLC
LaVergne TN
LVHW061947070526
838199LV00060B/4021